With Rhyme and Reason

*Intent, Inspiration
And
Historical Turns*

By **Sue k Green**

Printed by KDP Publishing
United States of America

With Rhyme and Reason

Copyright © 2019 Sue k Green

ISBN: 9781724035981
Independently published

Previous books of poetry by author:

"As Time Sneaks By"

"Love is Climbing the Rainbow"

"From my Heart"

"Storms of Stroke"

Additional poetry by author may be found on:

https://allpoetry.com/Sue_k_Green

About the Author:

Sue Green is a wife, mother, grandmother, poet, and photographer. Her poetry and photography give meaningful perspective to an otherwise chaotic world and speaks out on pertinent topics while creating a legacy of thought and inspiration for others.

She shares her poetry at monthly meetings of *'Poet's Corner,'* in the Monroe Township Library, Monroe Township, NJ.

"My lines of poetry are vibrations of my soul, crying out, touching others, raising awareness; rhythmic, though not always with rhyme, poetic, yet not always in standard form, telling yet not demanding, finding space, not stealing place.

My verse speaks with written message, calls out to cries of injustice, gives voice to personal as well as societal issues, opines on current conversation, and calls others to action. They are caring, concerned, and offered with reasonable process and thought."

Sue k Green

With Rhyme and Reason

Yesterday's memories
Today's fragmented thoughts
Tomorrow's tale

Table of Contents Page#

Table of Contents

Page#

With Rhyme and Reason

Worded with intent
Flowing with emotion
Rippled with thoughts

With Rhyme and Reason

With rhyme and reason
No remorse
The words committed
Find their course

Words that dance
With free expression
Oft' send out a
Thoughtful lesson

Words that hug me
Find my place
Whirred with wisdom
In time and space

Words released and
Safely spent
With rhyme and reason
Cause and lament

As Pages Turn

As pages turn in Book of Life
Chapters detail love and strife
Driving energy, inventive thought
Such daily tome that time has wrought

<u>Rivers of Verse</u>

Rivers of verse flow with rushing thoughts,
crash past emotional trappings and channels of controversy,
breaking through waves of conscience and ripples of
caution.

Streams of sentiment rush with winding course,
around curves of introspection toward banks of reason;
questioning, searching; settling in calming waters.

Breaking waves of consequential words,
reach out and crash with tides of confidence,
reaching sentimental shores.

Banks of awareness and inspiration find
course with rocky words and sands of thought,
all in rivers of verse.

<u>Shores of Resolution</u>

Poetry

rages with words, breaking down waves
of despair, drowning grief and loss, finding
consolation in healing verse.

flows through confusing thought
with stormy words and emotional swells,
calming with grounds of reason.

floats with rapture in the sea of love,
ripples in tales of family ties, finds
friendship in comforting places.

meets the wonders of nature,
with forests of adventure and
pathways to innovative thought.

stretches into time and place,
making reach into infinite space for
answers and understanding.

unwraps hidden dreams,
otherwise left unexposed
in the dark of night.

lights the day with morning sunshine,
promising rainbows of thought, and
filling stretches of time.

streams through challenges,
waves of distress, storms of emotion,
and searches for shores of resolution.

Expression Unearthed

A rhythmic write

Inky thoughts

Deliberate composition   Expressive outcry

Baring emotion

Emitting fears

Catching tears   Anger   Confusion

Happiness   Love   Caring

Shouting   Whispering

Unearthing concerns   Courting controversy

Giving light to dark thoughts

Provoking   Challenging   Searching

Finding resolution   Celebrating

Connecting   Sharing   Calming

Poetic verse

Expression unearthed

Embers

Words that burn like embers
Fall in verse from raging flames
Charred emotion chips

But scorched reflections
Escape their fiery finish
With poetic rescue

With Poetic Rescue

Words that feel, songs that sing,
tears that cry, are thus spoken with
verse to stand as monument in time,
circumstance, thinking, and intent.

Thoughts are expressed,
emotions are a bared, and
stories are told with candor,
for others to read and opine.

Readers may find personal relevance,
disagree in concept, search for further
understanding, or choose different
paths to follow.

<u>Behold the Artist</u>

Behold the artist's work on canvas
The craft formed of potter's clay

The rhythmic line of poetic thought
The stories writ and read each day

The quiet in the interlude
The empty space between
That focus on the 'little things'
That each day go unseen.

From hand and heart
Color and craft, deft design,
Musical composition, storied plot
Poetic verse, winsome rhyme.

Bursts of expression
Shape and fold
Noteworthy sounds
Tales now told

Take time to listen
Take time to hear
Such worthy a bundle
Is well worth a share.

Between the Folds

Between the folds of earth and sky,
life is borne.

Between the folds of light and dark,
days are spent.

Between the folds of nighttime dreams,
thoughts and fantasy play.

Between the folds of morning light,
challenges and opportunities rise.

Between the folds of challenge,
opportunities find way.

Between the folds of life and times,
pages are filled with stories told.

Between the folds of tales thus told,
emotions alight and imagination turns.

Between the folds of fantasy,
time and space reach meaningful expression.

A Promising Array

I needn't photograph my sorrow
Or paint away my tears
I'll just dream about tomorrow
And wish away my fears.

I'll watch the colors of the rainbow
Paint the sky just after storm
And see the sun when clouds have scattered
And happier times are borne.

In my dreams, there are no shadows
And flowered paths show me the way
As I think about tomorrow
In a promising array.

River of Time

Life on the River of Time
Currents of conflicts
Streams of challenge
Flooded with dreams

With eyes into space
Waves of curiosity
Tides of learning
Meaning, purpose

Surge of questions
Floods of theory
Time and space
Life finds place

All in a Splash of Time

Each morning
Morning light
Light and awakening

Awakening breath
A breath of awareness
Awareness of self

Self-entangled in time
Time entwined with space
Space clouded with questions

Questions without end
End far-reaching
Reaching for answers

Answers then chronicled
Chronicled with interpretation
Interpretation challenged

Challenged over time
Time affecting search
Search into space

Space, infinite in time
Time in limitless measure
Measured only by man

Man, life, mere ripples
Ripples in its stream
Stream in its measure

Measure of life
Life's spirit
Spirit and conscious

Conscious journey
From birth to death
Death, grief and loss
All in a splash of time

Only a Breath Away – Life and Death

Travelling the Traffic of Life

Mired in the traffic of life, moving forward on aging roadways and oppressive gridlock, sidelined by illness and death, friends and loved ones lost, weighted down with past memories, seeking course in busy lanes,

choking on rhetoric exhaust of powerful politicians who play chess with the lives and dreams of the people they promised to serve, crushed by broken dreams, school shootings, families in conflict, end of life stories,

stymied by misdirected signals, contradicting signs, road blocks to reason, curtailed by disparaging news, emotional trips, and unrelenting changes, straining to confront issues, adjusting lanes of thought, aching for clear passage,

one day at a time.

A Comforting Escape

On the table, sits a cup of mint tea,
yesterday's scattered mail, and
breakfast crumbs.

In my hand, an engaging novel,
a captivating story, and
a comforting escape.

Sunrise by the Sea

At first, the glint of light, pink hues on the horizon,
then, as if on cue, a ball of fire rises, its' reflecting
rays finding way to sandy shore.

The Last Blaze

As day folds into night
Earth basks in the golden glow
The last blaze of sunset
A scintillating, phosphorescent show.

So Distant, So Far

Away from all city light,
I watch from desert's sandy sight,
The stars so vivid, twinkling, bright,
So distant, so far; in the quiet of this night.

They Say

They say,
 tomorrow is not a promise, that today is a blessing.

They say,
death is an end to suffering, death is a peaceful journey.

They say,
there is light that guides past the darkness of death.

They say,
that love travels any distance even beyond our sight.

They say,
it is because of love that we feel so our loss.

They say,
grief is a journey and makes way to the healing.

They say,
it is only his body that has left my side,

They say,
that his spirit lives on in shared memories left behind.

They say,
in death, the essence of his soul makes touch
with other loved ones.

They say,
he is one with nature now.

They say,
he has only moved from one season to the next.

.

Lifetime of Memories

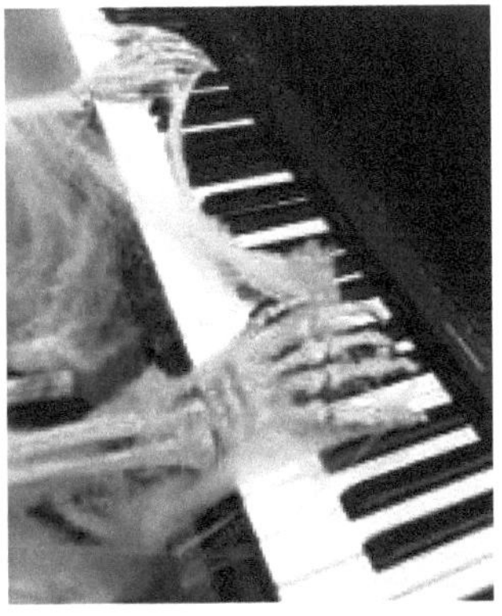

Death finds way to settle all debts
Grief makes final payment
As a keyboard of memories
Resound and replay.

Sitting on the edge of yesterday
Reaching for the present
Ghostly music is heard
As skeletal fingers play.

Striving to be at peace with
These visions and sounds
Of loved ones recently lost
And those long gone.

Voices, faces, shared bits of time preserved.

Miss you, bro…
Aaron Medinets, May you rest in peace.
9/22/1938-1/21/2019

Our Departed Loved Ones

When we rise up in the morning,
and we lay down in the night,
they are with us.

When seasons change,
leaves blow and flowers bloom,
they are with us.

At the beginning of a new year
and at its close,
they are with us.

When we are weary,
troubled, torn,
they are with us.

When we have joy
and wish to share,
they are with us.

At the start of new adventures
or in the excitement of completion,
they are with us.

When we have decisions to make,
and we draw on their lessons,
they are with us.

As long as we live,
we remember them, and
they are with us.

Inspired by prayer, "We Remember Them," by Sylvan Kamens and Rabbi Jack Riemer

Unload the Extra Baggage

Unload that extra baggage
Lighten up your load
Get rid your grief and anger
And walk straighter down that road.

Acknowledge,
Then release it,
Look forward, not to past;
And to today, commit.

No one can give you happiness
It's a present you give yourself
Train the brain, believe it
Keep negatives off your shelf.

> *Inspired by Rick Hanson's book, "Just One Thing - Developing a Buddha brain" one simple practice at a time.*

Only One Life

Only one life
  no minutes to spare;
    value your time,
      fill your days with care.

Dream your own dreams,
  find your own course;
    write on your timeline,
      with wonder and force.

Paved With Volumes

There is a path I know in the forest of adventure, paved with volumes of thought, filled with new friends, and crowded with consequence, and unimaginable intrigue.

Step carefully, for here every word is precious, every leaf inspiring, challenging.

It is an endless path, paged with the fruits of knowledge and shared thoughts and dreams.

It is an intriguing walk into other worlds, countries, and cultures.

It is anything but lonely.

Daily intake

Drinking green tea by the cup
Breathing deeply, in then out
Exercise routine, start slow
Diet watch, the way to go

Dust of Childhood

From the dust of childhood
grow limbs of enlightenment,
gardens of thought, forests of
understanding, and strong
branches of wisdom.

Faces worn

Masks that hide
And those so bold
Such are faces worn
Quarrel not the countenance
Unfolding there before you
Exhibit understanding
Reach to uncover
All which is hidden
Daylight unmasks
Exposes, emblazes

<u>One Byte at a Time</u>

Artificial Intelligence, making timely count,
syncing schedules, answering questions,
offering advice, promoting product, and
finding compatible mates.

Few resist this technological temptation that
gathers personal data, one byte at a time;
as it sits on desks, in cable boxes, slides
into pockets, and keeps watch on our wrists.

We do not want to admit that we are already
slave to its promises and victim to its potential.
Beep, buzz, and our eyes are on the screen.
All privacy has been surrendered.

With the sound of our voice or the tap of our finger,
it offers information, gives us reminders, counts
our steps, answers our questions, monitors
our travel and controls our reads.

Onscreen activity captures even the youngest
child. Texting seems to be the language of teens.
U-tube videos share personal captures and
singles are making new connections.

Devices are built into our dashboards mapping
easy to follow turn –by- turn directions while
keeping diary of our travel, pinging towers
with our every turn.

Is this the next step in the evolutionary process?
Programs to benefit mankind may be 'byting' up far
more than original intent and seem to be
growing beyond all expectations.

Virtual friends are found on Facebook,
Linked In, and Twitter, allowing info shares,
not in the safety of backyards and play parks,
while risking untoward seizure of personal data.

Social networks and competitive
computer games fill hours of time, and
supplant more rewarding physical activity
and personal conversation.

Texting is quickly replacing telephone calls
and casual conversation. Time has a way of
changing perspective, asserting new
meanings, and twisting trusted values.

Artificial intelligence is quickly
siphoning off the unique qualities
of our humanity, byte by byte.

HEY, SIRI

ALEXA,

ARE YOU LISTENING?

<u>"Don't 'hang me out to dry"</u>

Words that seemed omnipresent as oxygen have vanished
with scarcely a notice from our tongues, our pens and our
keyboards.

Words lost without nary a notice, styles changed at
designers' whim, and once common phrases losing
all meaningful reference.

Handwritten letters lie hidden in drawers,
undecipherable as foreign language to the
youngster hammering on his keyboard or
texting on his smartphone today.

Skinny jeans have replaced dungarees,
pedal pushers are now capris, and
Sketcher casuals and designer boots
have replaced saddle shoes and white bucks.

'Stoop' has given way to porch, patio, and deck,
'Rabbit ears' refer to animals, not TV antennas,
and 'don't touch the dial' replaced with
"Hey Siri, turn on the TV and shut off the lights."

'Hanging out to dry' and
'gone through the wringer' have
lost their reference, as clothes are
tossed quickly into the latest appliances.

'Typewriters' and 'carbon paper' have
been replaced with computers, spell check,
and electronic printers. Encyclopedias
have been shelved to 'Google searches.'

With Rhyme and Reason

Clouds of Storm
Seasons of Inspiration
Sunbursts of happiness
Rainbows of promise

The Earth has Music

Soft chorus with calming song
Crashing symphonies, discordant sound;
Close your eyes and listen
Nature's song is all around.

Roaring waves washing ashore
Their energy depleted
Yet back they flow, so life's concerto
In circles are completed.

Sun rising now above horizon
Light of day we see
At night the sky will darken
Nature's daily melody

I watch how the birds are soaring
Making quiet cadence in the sky
Orchestrated balance
I stand and watch and sigh.

Silent notes found in flowers
In blooming composition
Blended tones in color
Nature's musical rendition.

The gusty winds oft' challenge
Changing sands on my safe shore
Believing calm notes will follow
Keeps me in tune with nature's score.

But all now seems in harmony
As seasons make their change
Winter, summer, spring, and fall
A sight and sound exchange

Seasonal Shades

Pink cherry blossoms,
Purple crocus,
Yellow daffodils,
Red Spring tulips

Green lawns and new leaf cover
Warm **azure** waters
Sandy summer beaches,
Straw picnic baskets

Grey clouds
Summer storms
Brown splashy puddles
Fresh plant growth

Clear blue sky
Golden sunshine
Bright r**ainbows**
Warm, muggy air

Red and **gold** autumn leaves
Bare **brown** branches
Stringy winter clouds
White wintry snowflakes

<u>Spring Signs</u>

Ah, the blooming signs of spring!

Midst the wind and still cool days,
Spring keeps peeking in.
Daffodils withstand the gusts,
Magnolia blossoms bloom,
Lawns turn green, leaves appear,
And warm days filter in.

Summer Storm

Humid air hung heavy,
dark overcast chased
away the blue sky
and puffy white clouds.

The whirling winds sang
with frightening tone,
forewarning summer
storm's approach.

First small drops lead
to watery downpour,
bolts of lightning, and
thundering crashes.

In span of minutes only,
the angry storm was spent;.
bright sun and ravishing rainbow
chased 'way the dark clouds.

Such, the storms of summer!

Campfire Blaze

Called the Campfire Blaze…
seasonal drought, dry timber,
gusting winds, and a single spark
ignites the blaze.

The high winds spread new pockets of flame
and makes rapid path across California woodlands,
cities and towns. Evacuation orders are sent out.
Residents scramble to find safe ground.

Thousands of firefighters rush to the scene,
fighting hard to control the blaze which
has already been termed
California's deadliest wildfire.

Five thousand personnel fight the blaze
that has burned through 125,000 acres,
destroyed over 6500 hundred
homes and businesses.

Fires continue to spread. Over fifty lives
have been lost and the count continues
to rise as more charred remains will
undoubtedly be found in coming days.

As man interacts with nature, heroes are made and
lives are lost. Heavy rains, massive floods, drought,
and blustery winds, mark distinct weather changes,
and real threat of global warming.

<u>Wind Swept Leaves</u>

The wind swept leaves of color and hue
  propose new shade of nature's view.
To whirling sounds, they swiftly dance;
  the reds, the golds, downward advance.
I stand in awe as cool winds blow
  enfolded now in Fall tableau.

<u>Cold Snap</u>

Artic air
Blustering winds
Cold snap

Dress warm
Ear muffs on
Fashion set back

Good fun
Healthy play
Inches high

Jacketed children
Kicking the snow
Licking falling flakes

Measure the snowfall
Now that storm has stopped
Obsessed with numbers

Plows and shovels
Quickly clear
Roads and walks

Snow angels
Tracks in the snow
Unwitting tableau

Violent storms
Winds still blowing
XXX, out this forecast!

Yuletide storm
Zillions of white flakes

With Rhyme and Reason

Historical turns
Sounding alarms
Democratic Challenges

The Course of Democracy

From a wetland of ideas and ancestral thought,
democracy flowed.

Despite rocky patches, rivers of idea
channeled the way.

Ideas of freedom, equality, leadership,
and direction trickled forth.

A weighty river of thirteen states, fraught with human
refuge, sought better course.

From diverse waters of thought, compromising
direction flowed forth.

And the ship of Democracy anchored at our shore,
flying the red, white, and blue.

Harboring the Bill of Rights, the Constitution,
leadership, and right of vote.

Buoyed by years of challenge from those who
misinterpret intent and tear and shred the truth.

Flooded by the free speech of others who drown the
narrative with tidal waves of destructive intent.

Saved by the patriotic voices, strong leaders, independent
court rulings; the bulwarks of democracy.

This is America

A democracy always changing with the direction of vote,
turbulent at times, and tested by adversity.

Rooted in law, with governmental branches
designed with oversight, and paged with prudence.

Allowing for both controversy and compromise,
discourse and decision, change and resilience.

Standing tallest when strongest winds blow,
freedoms are challenged, and divisive rhetoric takes hold.

When the landscape changes, autocratic winds make storm,
waves of contempt are witnessed and deceptive grabs of
power occur.

This is a growing democracy, still learning how to stand
united, and instill freedom and equality in a world fraught
with challenge and diversity.

Few of Us Have Been So Tested

And so we say "Good-bye" to a true patriot
who served his country
with respect and honor.

As Navy veteran,
prisoner of war,
Presidential candidate,
six terms senator.

A maverick always,
marching to a tune
of values over party,
conscience over division.

Reaching right and left,
with compass true north;
facing forward, and
acknowledging failures,

Speaking out until
he could no more;
leaving a legacy for
others to follow.

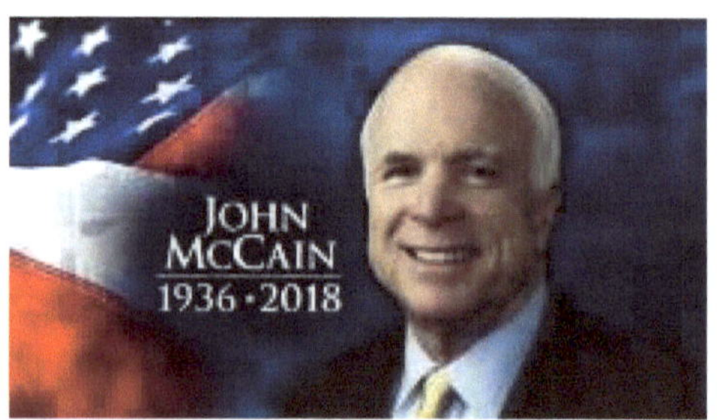

He loved his country
and served it well;
defended democracy
and left with no regrets.

Our country mourns.
American and foreign leaders
pay tribute, citing his courage
in ways few of us have been tested.

.

<u>Eulogy: George H. W. Bush</u>

"We don't want an America that is closed to the world.
  We want a world that is open to America."*

With grace and dignity,
he held the highest office.
With world partners,
he faced off the enemy.

With effort becoming
a true patriot, he
reached across the aisle
on so many fronts.

With promise, respect,
and understanding, he
appreciated his role
and America's diversity.

With sincere faith, straight talk, and deepest humility he
served this country and its people with accountability and
allegiance.

       *Quotation from George H. W. Bush
        Age at death: 94

Image credit for McCain and Bush photos: ww.google.com

Shelved

Shelved now are the political journeys,
patriotic ideals, and promises made in the past;
wrought of moral consciousness, ideas of
freedom, equality and an audacity to hope.

Pages of historical reference,
shelved for the leaders of tomorrow.

To Those Who Served

To those who served and came home broken
with war still rampant in their head,
gun shots waking them from sleep,
battles raging, and vivid visions
of their fallen comrades.

To those who struggle to find a place
in this land for which they fought,
and to those families stressing with
the disconnect of their loved ones' return,
We owe respect, honor, and support.

And to those who lost their lives,
we must honor their memories,
support their loved ones, and
try best to understand their loss.

<u>America's Tapestry</u>

The Statue of Liberty still stands tall, on an island in the harbor of our eastern shore.

"Give me your tired, your poor, Your huddled masses yearning to breathe free, The wretched refuse of your teeming shore."

*"Send these, the homeless, tempest-tossed to me, I lift my lamp beside the golden door."**

The words written there, opening our borders to others in despair. And so millions of immigrants from round the world entered and merged into America's tapestry.

The Lady still stands, the light of liberty in her hand, but the words, written still at eastern shore make no judgement on the color of skin, the accent in speech or from the direction one's flight has come.

Today, our country suffers with immigration squabbles, administrative confusion, lawlessness, and unrest. On our southern border, one finds walls and fences, family separation, delays, and deportations.

Our borders should be open, but need be guarded and protected from those who seek to harm and disrupt. Those who seek refuge here must respect our country, know and obey its laws, and learn to speak its' language.

Our immigration policies must be reviewed; not in the heat of racial rhetoric, but in the light of liberty. Our country, our freedom, and our humanity are at stake.

**"The New Colossus," patriotic poem by Emma Lazarus.*

For the Love of Money

For the love of money, many have gone astray,
compromised their souls, followed sordid paths,
and lost their way.

For the love of money, many have walked in
thick forests of despair and deceived friends,
unmindful of ultimate cost.

For the love of money, throughout
all the years, that quest has been made,
and dollars have bought 'friends.

For the love of money, friendships waver,
and crowds abide to await their share.

Enjoy the Beat

Many walk on by as
this musical troupe
plays to the
generosity
of the crowds that
gather.

I wonder the different
stories that prompt
this musical entourage; trying to reach others with a tap to
their beat.

The Forgotten

Found in city and suburb, those who
gather for warmth over ash can fires
before settling for the night on
hard earth beds.

They grovel on street corners,
begging for small change, as
city dwellers walk on by,
blind to their need.

Race, religion, and age find no barrier
where poverty and depression
lead to hunger, hopelessness,
and hapless crime.

The forgotten, a parcel and part of America's landscape

<u>On the March to Equality</u>

The month is not quite April
The year, 1858
Guests now have gathered
Not a one is late

The banquet's at the table
They drink the wine and eat the quail
Pretty faces on the ladies
Men in white shirt, coat and tail

Conversations easy
Polite, is how they say
Between the soup and beef stew
Kind words only on display

Now parted from the table
Gents together smoke
While women sit and chatter
Like cultured southern folk

While house slaves clean the table
As they have prepared the meal
The war had not begun yet
And slavery was real

The men talk of secession
The North is way too bold
The life that we have made here
Is fine and we must hold

But history tells the story
Of the war that was to come
How brave men fought the battles
And how so many did succumb

We and Them

White men reached this distant shore,
found natives farming, fishing, more.
With guns and slight they drove away,
took their land, kept them at bay.

Waves of immigrants, through the years,
reached our shores, by sweat and tears.
Liberty called, freedom for all; but
segregation, more often the call.

On the backs of immigrants, America grew
liberty and equality of an American brew.
Privileged classes, import of slaves,
child labor, this America knew.

In the house, with child, women had their place.
"Bear the children, serve the menfolk,
  keep a smile on your face."

Power and greed, cause conflict and clashes,
world wars, dominance, burning people to ashes.
We weep at the loss and the waste of it all;
yet from loud rhetoric, division's the call.

"Death to the infidels," and the Towers came down,
and we were embroiled in a Middle East town.
Islamic doctrine twisted and turned,
"We and Them" re-defined and concerned.

Immigrants on our southern border,
policy now quite out of order.
Refugees seeking asylum with cause; and
our leaders want walls and try skirting the laws.

Shots Fired

Me Too Movement
Black Lives Matter
White Supremacy Chants
Holocaust Deniers

Hate Crimes on the rise,
mass shootings in schools,
places of work, public gatherings,
and even in houses of prayer.

Such faces we wear, when mistrust ensues,
lies and false stories are covered as news,
power and greed are focused with deception,
and the face of America decries its conception.

Democrats, Republicans, concerned and distraught
answers and compromise, far from their thought.
"We and Them" here, there, and when,
even in God's name, again and again.

How Many Tears

How many tears must flow?
How many children fall?
How many senseless shots be fired?
How many parents must we watch cry out
Before we seriously address the cause?

Price of Freedom

Bought elections
Misinformed electorate
Unwitting choices

Vote validity
Inept leaders
Broken alliances

Damning discourse
Congressional inaction
American crisis

I have to believe
We will emerge strong
And from it take lesson

Hold accountable
Call them out, those who flout
Our rule of law and constitution

Words and guns are dangerous both
When acrimonious tensions mount
And divisive rhetoric shouts

Wake up, America
Take heed and hear the call

America can only be free
If we keep on alert, stay our allegiance,
Uphold our moral code, and hold high our flag.

Asylum Seekers 2019

And they marched across borders
Carrying pack and baggage

And they marched, hungry and tired
Clenching tightly frightened children

And they marched, with babes in their arms
Hope in their hearts, not knowing their fate

And they marched, looking for freedom
From guns, drugs, rape and hunger

And they marched, with so many others
Paying to and led by unsavory strangers

And they marched under harsh conditions
Mile after mile, amid the filth of travel

And they marched, day after day
Month after month, country after country

And they marched, alone, but yet with crowds
Hope fueling their steps with promise of asylum

And they reached their destination
The U.S. border, and were eager to cross

And they found at the border,
Long lines of ravaged refugees
Waiting for entry, their cries ignored

And they found at the border,
Delay and deflection
Fair process stalled

And they found at the border
Deception and separation
Cages and camps

And they found at the border
A political tinderbox
And they were pawns

And they found at the border
Asylum denied, mass deportations
Children separated from parents

And they found at the border
Disappointment, not promise
Politics at play, humanitarian crisis

Image from internet: credit John Burnet/NPR

<u>Creating Chaos</u>

Target the poor, the desperate, make powerful the rich.

Deny scientific facts.

Boost big business at the cost of National Parks, clean
waterways, and natural disasters.

Create border chaos, challenge democratic values,
promote loyalty, not experience.

Praise enemies, rebuke friends.

Twist truths, turn tides with
waves of discourse and self-praise.

Deny an unpropitious past, while covering up with
'alternative facts' and shifting blame to others.

Disavow the"#Me2" movement, the words and faces of
women, who dare now speak out.

Create diversion and chaos, day by day,
headline by headline.

Each story, redefining America, trampling legal and moral
values, stomping all opposing sounds.

Creating chaos one day at a time.

<u>In Crisis</u>

Words, bullets of abuse;
lies, slander, and fabrication finding the news,
wealth affecting power, power provoking division,
division producing leaders of doubtful conscience…

Freedom falls hostage when
rush for power condemns justice,
voice of opposition is crushed,
and filled with troublesome rhetoric.

"The pen is mightier than the sword,"
spoke Thomas Paine and with these words,
fanned the flames of revolution.

The cry of "Fake News" and denunciation of all opposition
from leaders in our highest levels of government place our
country in danger from both within and without.

These are difficult times. Truth is often lost in the rush to
headlines. Outlook, too, is often clouded by bad judgement
and promise of personal gain.

Words grow now as dangerous as guns; assault weapons in
schools and streets, cars and trucks exploited as weapons.

Our freedoms, our democracy, and our stand in the world
of nations are in crisis.

Hauntingly Familiar

Familiar words as history turns
Excesses, overreach, appeasement
Hate groups, division, blame

Frightening childhood memories in a war-torn world of
displacement, corruption, and powerful change.

How hauntingly familiar to holocaust survivors,
todays' divisive rhetoric and disregard for rule of law.

In old age, it rouses memories and they speak out,
hoping the world will listen and understand.

And the Alarm Rings

With silent condemnation and ignorance, divisive
discourse, and disregard for rule of law…

With alternative facts weighing heavy over truth and
equality, and partisan politics stifling progress…

When the poor are forgotten, the middle class is displaced,
corruption becomes an acceptable reckoning and the rich
wield all powers of state…

<u>But Democracy Will Stand</u>

when the press purposes truth, citizens stand up, speak out,
and take action.

when wrongs are righted and solidarity sounds speak
to American values of freedom, equality, and morality.

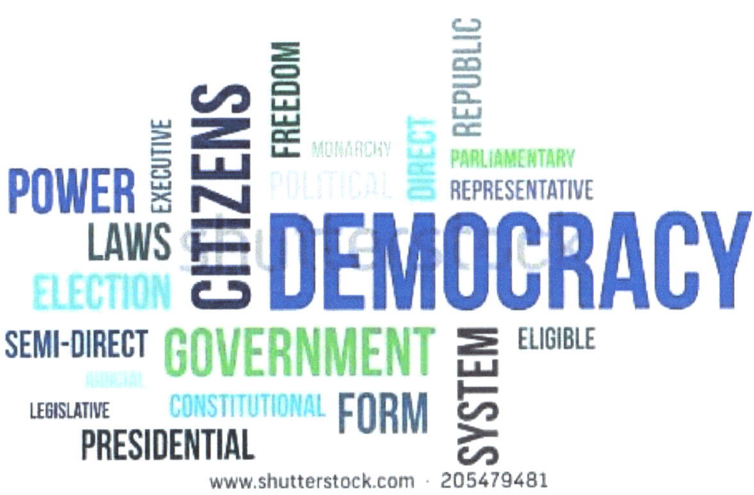

Clip art credit for images pg. 44, 49, 50